Praise for *Kind*

"It is this poet's calling to hold kindness and its opposite in tension. What is that opposite? The poems in this volume offer unsettling answers. With Gretchen Primack's poems, the absence of kindness causes a quaking in our bodies. A lyrical language of the present tense evokes a fierce and tender impatience with what should never have been settled for."
—**Carol J. Adams**, author of *The Sexual Politics of Meat*

"This book is essential reading. Read these poems for the truth they tell about our relationship to and treatment of the creatures we take to be our property; read this book and ponder its many questions, for example 'Who are the beasts?' and 'What can I do?'"—**Kazim Ali**, author of *The Voice of Sheila Chandra*

"*Kind*—an unassuming, everyday word, a word sprung from the Old English *kin*, meaning *family*—stitches this book together because each poem herein is an aching missive written to animals, poems of love and protest that refuse to bow down to our order of what is worthy and what is less than, to separate what is 'born for love or commerce,' to set apart what is human versus not. Each poem dissolves and reshapes these divisions with inexhaustible empathy and a ferocious determination that pleads—yea, even demands—kindness for all living beings."—**Nickole Brown**, author of *To Those Who Were Our First Gods*

"How often does one get starstruck by a poet? When I read Gretchen Primack's animal poems, I was starstruck instantly. How could someone crystallize my own feelings about animals and humanity so beautifully, so powerfully, and so poignantly?"—**Marisa Miller Wolfson**, filmmaker of *Vegucated*

"Gretchen Primack is infused with an abnormal amount of empathy, which fills her heart with kindness, awe, and hope. She wants to live 'somewhere else, somewhere kind,' so she spends her time shifting into that place where every being matters, and she takes us with her."
—**Sharon Gannon**, author of *Magic is a Shift in Perception*

kind

poems

GRETCHEN PRIMACK

Lantern Publishing & Media • Brooklyn, NY

2021
Lantern Publishing & Media
128 Second Place
Brooklyn, NY 11231
www.lanternpm.org

Front cover painting: *Disguise* (2015) by Dana Ellyn
Cover design: Gus Mueller and Nancy Leonard
Author photo: Deborah Degraffenreid

Printed in the United States of America

Library of Congress Cataloging-in-Publication Data

Names: Primack, Gretchen, author.
Title: Kind / Gretchen Primack.
Description: Brooklyn, NY : Lantern Publishing & Media, [2021] |
Identifiers: LCCN 2020050869 (print) | LCCN 2020050870 (ebook) | ISBN 9781590566398 (hardcover) | ISBN 9781590566404 (epub)
Subjects: LCGFT: Poetry.
Classification: LCC PS3616.R545 K56 2021 (print) | LCC PS3616.R545 (ebook) | DDC 811/.6—dc23
LC record available at https://lccn.loc.gov/2020050869
LC ebook record available at https://lccn.loc.gov/2020050870

For Gus:
My kind,
my beloved,
my kind beloved

and for our
Sally and Eleanor

human is neither
wiser
nor more blessed

—Lucille Clifton

the patience
of the universe
is not without
an end

—Lucille Clifton

CONTENTS

About the Author
About the Artists
About the Publisher

ACKNOWLEDGMENTS

Some of these poems have appeared in:

Borderlands: Texas Poetry Review ("Phoebe Fledges")
Cortland Review ("Hall Farm")
Defeffable ("Coxcomb")
FIELD ("Picnic")
Innisfree ("The Absence of Unnecessary Hurting," "Eccentric")
Jewish Currents ("Taste It," "The Other Half of the Simile," "The
    Dogs and I Walked Our Woods")
The Poetry Distillery ("Apes, May I Speak to You a Moment?")
Project Intersect ("Big Pig," "Mother I," "Mother II," "The Workers")
Spoon River Poetry Review ("Don't Let Him Be Lonely")
Terrain: ("Fawn")
The Same ("Purple Milkweed I," "Purple Milkweed II")
46millionturkeys.com ("Thanksgiving")
Zoomorphic ("Chain," "Ringling")

"The Dogs and I Walked Our Woods" was also included in three
anthologies: *Riverine: An Anthology of Hudson Valley Writers* (Codhill Press,
2007), *Dead Animal Handbook* (2015), and *Ghost-Fishing: An Eco-Justice
Poetry Anthology* (2018), and reprinted in *Project Intersect* #2.

"Love This" was reprinted in Carol J. Adams's *The Sexual Politics of
Meat*, 25th anniversary edition (Bloomsbury, 2015).

I am deeply grateful to Dayl Wise and Alison Koffler of Post Traumatic Press, whose graciousness, compassion, and skill brought the original *Kind* into the world.

Dana Ellyn's cover art, as well as interior images from Gus Mueller, Jane O'Hara, and Dana, profoundly deepen the impact of this book. I am proud to know these artists and beyond grateful that they share their work here.

I am so appreciative of Lantern Publishing's Martin Rowe and Brian Normoyle. Their faith in this book, and their vision, mean the world.

Thank you, fellow vegan poets, for your inspiration, including: David Alexander, Kazim Ali, Ashley Capps, Allison Davis, Ross Gay, Gabriel Gudding, Chloe Hanson, Ananda Lima, Dimitri Reyes, and Donald Vincent (Mr. Hip).

Great love to fellow writers whose support and feedback through the years has meant so much: Carol J. Adams, Bruce Beasley, Celia Bland, Nickole Brown, Sarah Browning, Kia Corthron, Ruth Danon, Randall Horton, Joan Larkin, Tom Lux (RIP), Wendy Wilder Larsen, Ethelbert Miller, Vijay Seshadri, Tim Seibles, and David Young.

FOREWORD

Tim Seibles

Kind is a collection of poems that wants something from us, something troublesome but essential if we hope to be fully awake in our lives. Attentiveness comes at a price, of course. Undoubtedly, there are questions we'd prefer to avoid, territories of thought we'd rather not enter, but this is a critical feature of what poetry does, what *Kind* does—takes us by the hand, sits us down, then asks, *what about this and this and this?*

These poems insist that we read with our eyes wide open—perhaps the way we walked into kindergarten—half-excited, half-scared by what we might come to see, to learn. Both our innocence *and* our complicity concerning the lives and deaths of animals are frankly scrutinized; this is what amplifies the poignance of Gretchen Primack's work. While reading this collection, I couldn't help but recall the many years I enjoyed my mother's cooking—chicken, pork chops, hamburgers, hot dogs—with no understanding that these *foods* were parts of the bodies of once living creatures. At the same time, I was obliged to confront my current willingness to turn away from what I *do* know about all we eat.

As a city boy, I had no notion of animals being killed for my nourishment. I would have just as soon believed meat came from meat trees. I certainly had no grasp of the machinery of slaughterhouses nor, for that matter, any knowledge of what a dairy farm really did to get all that milk. Most of us who were not raised on farms grew comfortably into this ignorance about our *daily bread*. Perhaps parents simply meant to protect us from the long shadow of our predation—or maybe they had learned to bury this knowledge to protect themselves.

Surely, some conflict with the rest of the living community is unavoidable. When we clear land for farming, when we clear land for our towns and cities, highways and airports, we destroy the creatures whose lives on those many, many acres preceded human interest. Primack understands this, yet her poems comprise a clear invitation, an unmistakable imperative, to become truly conscious of the animals we consume—as well as those we enlist for circuses and zoos to add to our catalog of entertainments.

William Carlos Williams wrote, "It is difficult to get the news from poetry, but men die every day for lack of what is found there." Gretchen Primack might well amend that to include *the entire living community* of animals, plants, and insects, all of which are vulnerable given the lack of news about them. In a persona poem, "Holstein," a cow used for dairy asks her child to "put your head where your kind / is never allowed: at my flank." With imaginative dexterity and soulful pleading, this entire collection compels us to think the *un*sanctioned thoughts, to look where we seldom dare.

The author understands that we must wrestle with the ideas that have bent the world and, finding our lives misshapen by its common cruelties, try to transform ourselves, so that we do not witlessly sustain a status quo that, ultimately, serves no one. Even those who may never be vegan will be awakened by this book—as will anyone who believes that a kinder world would be a better place for *all* living things.

Tim Seibles is the author of several poetry collections, including *Hurdy Gurdy, Hammerlock, Buffalo Head Solos,* and *Fast Animal,* which was a finalist for the 2012 National Book Award and winner of the Theodore Roethke Memorial Poetry Prize. Tim is a former NEA fellow and recipient of a fellowship from the Provincetown Fine Arts Work Center. His latest collection, *One Turn Around the Sun* was released in 2017. He recently completed a two-year appointment as poet laureate of Virginia.

Picnic

Peas snug in their sweet green
coats, tea snug in its thermos,
absolutely orange tomatoes. Mice
root and clack and fill
their little lungs, each eye bright
as a berry. It is easy to forget Hell
here, and that is what we talk about:
Hell, and forgetting it. Once
I tried to save a bee, named
and cared for and cried for the bee.
In this plot curl the brown brain
rills of rows of seeds almost ready
and seeds spent. I'm tired of it all
being about life and death. We are
navel-gazy, a couple of Uncle Vanyas
woe-ing and alas-ing our way through
middle life. I've dressed this salad
before, searching for people who Get It
while drops pock the pond and
the pincushion of the garden.

It is still Sunday after all this time;
this Sunday is as long as March.
We need to hear our hearts to feel alive,
sometimes in a bitter way, sometimes
a lovely way, hear them too fast
and too hard in order to feel alive.
This might be why people hurt so many
so often: to hear the hearts of the scared
makes hearts beat fast.

No, mice, you are not this way. No,
bees, you are not, dogs, pigs, hens.
But we are, and you are
at our mercy. You cannot forget
Hell for even a day, and so I cannot
either.

The Absence of Unnecessary Hurting

This is the press of the earth. One star hanging
there, honking like a goose. The lake
a smudge of black juice, the hill a draped
pancake. Frogs singing, sharp
and gutty.

Night! Clean air, clear water, five
baby mink in a pile, snoring.
Overwhelm can be dug from sludge
below dock, on either side fruits slung
over branches, glued to their seeds.
Here in the slurry live the things
I consider, here in the hills. What do people
think of? What do they think of me
in my carings?

Ripples lunch on each other, heavenly
body lights flicker, too cool for moths.
I don't want to hurt things.
The fine brown eye of an animal,
the broad slick leaf of a wing.
I'd like to be gentle here.
I want to be worthy of you, lovely
ground, bury my face in your tired
broken bread.

Dana Ellyn, *Pattern Chicken*

Coxcomb

Here was where
the bully could not reach.
        —Greg Kuzma

Abraham was a rooster. He'd been made to fight. He was not a
        fighter.
He ended up in a basement with a "No one touch the killer!"

We brought him to the sanctuary. He loved peanut butter and jelly.
He loved laps and Linda's pillow. He was not a fighter. He wanted

to be held by toddlers, phi beta kappas, grievers and
socialists and pop stars. He wanted you to gentle his comb

between your forefinger and thumb. It was a smooth, warm piece of a
smooth, warm Abe, and it blushed bliss. It was tender

like someone who had been as unloved as a chicken
and then as loved as a chicken could be.

He grew old and full of love and died, rubbing his head back
and forth, back and forth against Linda's arm. We planted

coxcomb, a growing glow.

THE DOGS AND I WALKED OUR WOODS,

and there was a dog, precisely the colors of autumn,
asleep between two trunks by the trail.
But it was a coyote, paws pink
with a clean-through hole in the left,
and a deep hole in the back of the neck,
dragged and placed in the low crotch
of a tree. But it was two coyotes,
the other's hole in the side of the neck,
the other with a dried pool of blood below
the nose, a dried pool below the anus,
the other dragged and placed
in the adjoining low crook, the other's body
a precise mirror of the first. The eyes were closed,
the fur smooth and precisely the colors
of autumn, a little warm to my touch though the bodies
were not. The fur was cells telling themselves
to spin to keep her warm to stand
and hunt and keep. It was a red
autumn leaf on the forest floor, but
it was a blooded brown leaf, and another, because
they dragged the bodies to create a monument
to domination, to the enormous human,
and if I bore a child who suffered to see this,
or if I bore a child who gladdened to see this, or if
I bore a child who kept walking, I could not bear
it, so I will not bear one.

MATTER

What if you were tiny:
a bit. A mote. What if
you were a grain, a green
grain waiting.
What if a fish
mattered as much as you
matter—if you do.

The men we are
might just wring our hands.
The men we are might pull
the moon from its space,
burn ourselves on it.

We are dying every day
and know it, each foot
wrapped in its shoe,
each train wrapped
in its tunnel, each lemon
blooming on a hill's belly.

Even so, I saw a cherry browning
in the dirt, moon orange
on the edges
and just as pocked,
and its loveliness was so painful
I wanted to put it in my mouth.

Suns are setting all over
the universe, beating down,
and we see just the one
little one.

Ringling

Maybe someday you will trick
for me.
Maybe I will find value in you
on one foot.

I will take you from family,
home,
so I can watch you
balance.

Will you bore me? I bore myself
now, reduced
to your conditions, cut off
from my life

and language. None of me
is left; still
you found something
to waste.

Gus Mueller, *Family*

ECCENTRIC

ek–out of
kentros–center

Dangling from the center's ledge.
Leaning on the center to nudge it over.
Stroking the center's back, weeping.
Staring cross-armed at the center.
Heaving a shroud over it.
Walking away until the center disappears.

Covid I

This year spring and summer decided
to go on without us,

to roll in the fields while we rolled
in poison—the glory! The relaxed

breaths of it! They pressed
against each other, not a reed fit

between, they made us wait
while the birds built and snakes sunned

and crocs snapped
at their frogs. The air milded

and cleared far from our sickbeds
because of our sickbeds.

O human, see, you are important—
Biology, hubris, apocalypse;

cages, carbon, energy—just
not the way you think. Just not

the way you wish.

Love This

If you permit this evil, what is the good
of the good of your life?
        —Stanley Kunitz

The body floods with chemicals saying, Love this,
and she does, and births it; it is a boy
she begins to clean and nose, but he is dragged
away by his back feet. She will never touch him
again, though she hears him howl and calls back
for days.

Her breast milk is banked for others. Her son
is pulled away to lie in his box.
He will be packed for slaughter. How ingenious
we are! To make product from byproduct:
make use of the child,
kill and pack and truck him to plates.

And when her gallons slow, we start over,
and her body says, Love this! And she does,
though in a moment she will never touch
him again. His milk is not for him.

And when the milk slows too slow,
she will join him on the line, pounds
of ground. How we will dine!
And talk of our glossy dogs! Her body
will break up on our forks, as mothers
beg us for the grain we stuffed her with,
and children beg us for the water
scouring her blood from the factory walls.

And when her wastes and gases and panic
heat our air so hot our world stops
breathing—then will we stop?
Then will we grow kind,
let the air cool and mothers breathe?

Dana Ellyn, *Veal*

GOD'S GLORY

With what shall we pay our entrance into an exclusive
Paradise, from which the beaver and the ant are barred?
           —Edna St. Vincent Millay

You would scoff at those who care
for small things. The mouse you killed.
Only, aren't you small,

your soft chest and your skull
balancing
on its skeleton?

I wish there were a God,
a mighty, hoary He showing
you are as small
as a brown mouse, whose home
you fastened upon

and whom you killed there.
I wish an awesome God
could show you what is small.

Gus Mueller, *I Think I Just Saw One*

Purple Milkweed I

Stamp your foot, cricket. You know enough.
There's an awful lot of leaning in this field,
every time one of the winds says *yes*.
Hard not to admire the unison, and the bristling
thistles, none of them lonely. This bloom least of all,
with its five flipped cones full from half a drop
of juice, pushing out strings almost invisible
to my awkward eye. A good forty cluster into a ball,
a good four balls cluster on a single stalk—
so many cones and shoots lounging in juice,
and none of it needs me.

Climate Change

A compass is always right, and I thought adults
were like that.   They would Figure It Out.

They would tremor in a shift and then true
us.   I grew into this world and its blood

factories.   Now I know only a compass
is a compass.   I don't like things hanging

over me so am anxious to get dying over with,
but I want all this other trauma,

this solvable hell, to get solved
and now.   But there are no adults

in that room.   They are busy
on the kill line.

And which of these lines
would slow that line for even a moment—

Puppeteer,

he doesn't want to be meat.
He didn't ask you to feed

what is wrong for him:
corn, a sawdust dim

in his belly, a mash of cramp
and gas.

He didn't tell you to plow
cloudforest to grow

that harm grain.
Puppeteer, pain

master, look at the living
limbs on your strings,

the cells in conference
to create his arced lens,

glossed flank, the
hard horn of each foot,

that deft design you
mad-scientisted into

unreal, useful,
dead.

ELEANOR

I loved all of you, even the cancer
in your neck and blood.

Even the sick mirror.
Your black fleece, white
cells, your bright red ones.
The lymph and sera
and your soft black mouth.
All the elbowing cells keeping
us up for each other
a little longer.

I humble before the system
that built our illnesses,
built your dog bones one by one
and tied them together
until you could walk toward me.

The system that filled them
with pocks round as zero,
pox tough as hide.

Let us walk toward
each other until our faces
touch.

COVID II

Who was the pangolin,
caged
in the truck, in the stack,
in the market

What could her body,
balled protection no protection,
smooth nail scales no protection,
do but uncurl and mark us

When did her cage unstack
from the hens above,
the pig below, the dog
alongside

When did hands pull
her smooth balled body and slit
her throat for its tonic blood,
cut her tissue for the pleasure
of meat

Where moved the first virion
in her body—eye, neck,
heart—
did its twisted ladders

course a thousand times,
a million through the mouths
of her cells before the hand
came down on her neck

(And the pig below,
the hens above,
what poisoned cells
course through their dread)

How do we fill our bodies
without her body, the hens
above and the pig below
and the dog alongside, leave

their lives and deaths
alone,
leave their cells alone
Why can't we

To tear someone from her life,
to cage her, to let her blood
for our habit—
did we imagine no consequence

Do we see it now

Mercy

I say we had better look our nation searchingly
in the face, like a physician diagnosing some deep disease.
        —Walt Whitman

Evil is alive
and feeds on our
fattened lambs.

Evil is thriving
and stuffed with
stuffed hens

until she is sleek
as a bird. Our mouths
are glossed with fat.

Leave your gods
at the door:
there is no room here

for even one. Milk
is blood and blood
milk, red and white,

white and red
as a bruise,
as sick, as a tear.

Oh, but you can close
every door, snap
the blinds in the house

of you; you can wrap
your gut in burlap
and string,

in polyethelene,
and the voice
still calls

Mercy.
It should not
have to beg.

It is a feather
itch, sometimes
a sore,

a thread,
a hot seed.
Mercy.

Even our easy wants
can't damp it.
Even evil.

SABLE

I'm cozy in your skin.
You were alive when
they took it, I saw
your muscle stripe
and glint and then
I saw you blink.

But I am rich
in your skin:
and rich means
worth.
So it is worth
your caged
crazed months,
the electric anal
stun, the wrench

of skin away from
muscle, the tossed
body. And after all
this, the blink.

Jane O'Hara, *Fox's Sleep*

Vermont I

Scared and stretched-smiling,
quaking in a vat of thunder like
you wouldn't believe.
Angry cracks seizing pacemakers
and pulling out teeth all over
town. My tight little house
is a tin thimble, its white wood
walls trembling in their cup.

Come in mice, red bugs, clack
beetles, come hear safe the shocked
hollers. You are not alone,
and neither am I alone.
You are not alone. I am not.
You make me thirsty, yellow storm.

VERMONT II

Thunder and thunder and no
rain. Thunder and no lightning
and no rain. Finally rain, coming,
coming.

I shush everything the better
to hear it, and take off my shoes
the better to feel you, my dear.
Fall in the green of the gloam,
having tired the thunder and the clicks
of light with your fall and
fall, dirty as a dollar, clean
as a nun. Warping the panes,
not knowing how to love me back,
or even sigh. Thunder! Heaven
havoc! Coming, coming, coming,
came.

VERMONT III

So much rain—
it just isn't natural.
The herons are bothered:
no luck with dinner, no
luck with lunch.

And when the hailstones frogjump
the grass, rushing the birds
and newts inside,
the flirting sculptors run
for cover under a red umbrella,
and I want to say,
Just get to bed already.

Brothers Grimm hailstones, look at them:
lovely, unlonely eggs in the grass.

FACTORY FARMS I

Inexcusable, the slaughter in this world.
Insufficient, the merely decent man.
　　　　　—Stephen Dunn

I giggled through Holocaust films—
what could I do with that in the basement
of the synagogue with the other fed
kids, what could we do with it, hell
and hell and us, suburbans introduced to
hell. They taught and taught, hammered us
that people said, *Everyone Is Doing It*
and then *How Was I Supposed to Know?*

During slavery they said,
It's Too Entrenched to Be Dissolved.
In Jim Crow times: *It's Just How We Do,
Who We Are.* Child labor:
It Makes Things Affordable.
On battered women, beaten kids,
*It's None of Your Business.
Leave Me Alone.*

The Workers

An undocumented immigrant,
an illiterate mother,
a hungry thirteen-year-old,
and a sadist
walk into a slaughterhouse.

It's the first rung
of the American ladder,
says the first.

Wal-mart's done hiring,
says the second.

School's not working,
says the third,
and neither is Dad.

A place, says the last,
where I won't be
punished.

The first sees the pig's
leg dislocate as she's hung:
Physics.
He feels it in his own leg.
He feels her blood
down his neck.

The second feels the chick
tremble as she sears off
his beak with a hot
blade.
She feels it in her
face.

The third did not know a cow
could make that sound,
the death sound he now knows
he will make one day.

The fourth slams
a chicken against a wall.
And again. The fourth sits
his weight on a calf too sick
to stand. Shoves his
finger up into a turkey
again and again.

The first has his arm caught
in a machine.

The second has a finger cut
off along a beak.

The third can't leave
his room.

The fourth slams a chicken
against the wall. Grinds

his heel into a turkey.
Shoves his fist up

into a calf again
and again—

Heron

I love the hand as well as the mind.
— Gerald Stern

Well, blue chicken, where is your bed?
You must be thinking with that neck.
I think with the meat and bones
that make my hands.

The light's lying thick as wheat paste on the water,
warm as a nest of sweat bees. Nothing about you
says *lonely*, and I'd like to kiss the side of your head.

Sure as the skin's stretched over me, I'm halfway
done. Certain things won't happen again,
certain lasts and firsts. Here on the bank grow
the first white muscle of an egret, a trillium's
first red tooth.

It is alright that I know so little
and will leave the world and all
its hands and twigs,
overlapping beaks, hearts and buds.

It's hard to keep thinking
about belonging and damage. Let
me go, blue bird, brown water.

Phoebe Fledges

This is for their mama, who left them
the only way she would have: by
dying.

And for the two who could not live
that way. And for the two who tried,
and cried out,

and for my husband, who heard
and hung the nest high in the house,
who knew what would happen

and fed them anyway,
through the night, through
the mites and shiverings,

and who buried them in their nest,
my kind love who loves
so hard.

HUSBAND

Now that's a leg even I would eat.
And those Maurice Sendak feet,
those filthy Wild Thing toes
in the woods and the workshop
and the bottom of the bed—those
are drumsticks even I'd fry up.

What about that boule of a biceps?
The color of a toasted boule,
it could toast
from the heat of my cheek
alone.

And when I slide my ear
to your chest I can hear
that your heart is as sweet
as a kitchen of cake.

Those eyes are two crocks
of bluestone, which none
among us eats, but which snails
pressed themselves into
in the small hours of life,
and which you come bursting in
to show me.

And this is why I'd like to unfurl
and swallow
the plump noodle of your brain:
because its left side says,
Brachiopods, early Cambrian,
and its right side says,
Let me show my love.

Mother I

I wouldn't make a sound if I wasn't so angry
I wouldn't be running if there weren't so far to go
—Ben Sollee, "Only a Song"

She is to mother yogurt.
She is to nurture cheese.
Curdle her milk into sour
cream. Call her mother.

She is denied her child
so we may suckle.
Her child is a chop
so we can serve

her milk to our children.
Always there is her child—
in her cells, in her udder,
the *yes* before the *no*

each time a machine is clamped
to her chafed breast.
Each element of the milk
is designed to raise him—

this is what the world
told her, her body told her,
and he came as promised,
and then the violence.

Big Pig

(In this way) we are going nowhere,
to survive like this holds no glory.
—Pablo Neruda

I want to talk to the pigs.
—Pablo Neruda

Big pig, smart and fattened
to grotesque, I am not better
than you, though I am different:
I can speak rage. I can
build your crate.
You reason like a preschooler,
but he can ask for ham,
and a mother oblige.

Pig, you will not see a sun in your life.
You will not know space
or mother. They will fatten you
on harrowing and hang you by a foot.
They will hack your neck
and you will struggle until your body
tears from its leg, and your foot
unleashes from its strap, and you pitch
to your own thick blood. And the man
with the knife, in his sadness,
he will kick and kick you,
and the ten after you, and the ten after,
the ten and ten after, speaking his rage:
Die, heartbreaking beast.

Dana Ellyn, *Piggy*

"Humane" I

I know a knife when I see one.
I want my throat whole.
What could I barter for my
self?

There is grass here.
Still, I want my throat.
There is the rope, the winch.
I want my life
like life does.

It isn't yours.

"Humane" II

To kill me
quietly
to kill me
swiftly
the strongest bolt gun
the sharpest knife
the cleanest floor

is violence

and fear
will trap in
every cell
of my self.

Because You Are Silver,

because of your round eye

and where it sits

because of your water home,

your air distrust

because fins are frilled paper   not hands,

because of your temperature

I can take your body,

hook you up in a flail

net you up with a thousand others

and no person will sigh for your   life,

Gus Mueller, *Happy Tilapia*

the body made for its home

just as any body is,

its flashing silver, its cool fins

and perfect eyes.

Because our vaunted minds

are too small to understand   other minds,

we will call you mindless

and swallow you.

Let me look that face

in the eye and tell you, fish,

I could no sooner eat your flesh

than my own.

Dining

His eyes thrill above the glass clink,
the shrink of muscle on your
plate smothered in aromatics masking
blood, wine masking blood. Breaking
bread, breaking bodies plucked halfway
to cremation by tongs from a grill.
That tongue will touch his tongue,
you use that tongue to pull in muscle,
you use that mouth to kiss, to form
love and *sweet* and *miss*, now to moisten
this, to swallow chunks, pull them
down tube after tube of you until their waste
is waste, for a quick, quiet taste of muscle
weeping onion, tissue weeping wine.

HOLSTEIN

I was also a child.
And also had one.
And another a year after.
And another.
And could not touch

even one.

Had I been born
into a kind world,
my life would have been
mine, not a stranger's,
as long as my body wanted life.

Had I lived in a kind world,
child, this milk would have been
yours. No one would have filled
your lungs with loss.

Put your head where your kind
is born to be
but is never allowed: at my flank.
The great spill of me. Smell me
from your bent neck. Child.

Jane O'Hara, *Blue Ribbon*

WHEN I GOT THERE THE DEAD OPOSSUM LOOKED LIKE

a sleeping prince. He didn't want a majestic
burial as majestic burials are inane. He wanted

his family back. He wanted to live but
we wouldn't let him. There were sweets to buy
and his route crossed ours so we crossed

him out. Nothing we could do then, and still
some middle-aged lady gathered him in her arms
and keened, his cold nose in her ear. Keening

is inane. His family wanted him, but there were ribs
to buy and manifest destiny.
I pressed his cheek to my cheek, stupid.

I pressed his head to my heart,
dumb.

REST

I am impatient for grief.
Not my usual kind, my grief
for the voiceless and hurt
in the world,

but the kind that will be thrown
at me when I suffer the loss
of someone I have loved
who I will have lost.

It will push aside my grief
of the ill-treated,
of being carried into the soot
with the hapless and cruel
and kind alike, all
of us destroyed,
some suffering more
along the way.

I'm tired
of this kind.
The new grief will rest
on me and let me
rest.

The Hunter

He cut trenches through the bluestone,
angled scraps littering land, stepping
stones to baby pines, welcome mats
to mullein. The trenches bear building
things to and fro, plans and boards
and sump pumps. The trenches bear
having been built, the landscape
bears them up, the mullein bears them.
The scape is not clever, but it is cut
and will start its reseeds right now.
It will start a thin, patient green, in
cross section a thin, patient line,
crackful of dirt seeding and a crack again.

He might as well talk to this rock, since
he is on it now and will be under it soon
enough. The rock fits a sharp horn
of rock under his thigh. Someday he will be
a sharp horn under a thigh, he thinks, though
he also thinks, *World, you are only good now
in the ways you are good for me.*

His body is on the rock. His mind is where
minds are, minds that think about where
time leaves bodies. He closes his eyes
and bays at the sun. Sometimes, not ready
for dropped leaves dropped dead, he thinks
about the rock he'll be under soon—soon
because everything is relative—and the rock
he will become, if that is where biology
and geology merge. Maybe he will become oil.

Now the air is blue as a cold day,
and all the holes in his head receive it,
and he howls at the sun breaking open.
But his gunshots are louder than howls,

a shooter crying into his animal,
Your life is mine now, so I have more life.
There is only one way out of this world
no matter the trenches, the buckshot. Still
he says, *When I take your life I take on life.*

Nothing is trying to hurl him or this rock
into space, but the leaves have begun to
drop, and his skin has its patterns now,
its new trace-paper feel, and his hair
travels in new strange patterns. So
there are his gunshots: *When I swallow
you, I swallow life.* He closes his eyes.
Maybe he will become rock,
maybe oil, a crack of soil, seeding.

WRUNG

I don't sleep, but you do—and perfectly.
The blind slats are tight, dogs and legs settled,
but my doze is thick and bruised. Meanwhile,
a face away, the breath you breathe
has wrung itself from you, and it is clean as hay,
as pie, as a sun. How that can fail to calm
I cannot figure, though I figure all night in half-
dreams by the Niger, drowning, weaving between
bullets, stricken creatures, deathbedded friends, stricken
creatures on a loop on a loop until it is wrung out
like breath, the space between thoughts. Meanwhile,
a face away, the breath you have pulled up is clean
as poppies. It smells like growing.

APES, MAY I SPEAK TO YOU A MOMENT?

May I apologize? For the man holding us all
on strings, he of the red face, thinning hair,
he of the death of love and fear of death?
He of the foot stamp, crow bar, backhoe? He
of the better than, contortions, slick definitions blue
with torsion? He of the ex lax, immodium, tums
for the tum-tum? Milk of magnesia, milk of cow,
milk of bull? Apes, may I be sorry though I crumple
below my strings, never pull hard enough or make
the cuts? Though I dance for him as much as you?

MARIE

Here is an old cat, a lump
on my lap, a wisp, a *shirrup*
on the world, a center
only to me, myself only
a *shirrup* on the world, a wisp
of lint in its long afternoon.
Her cat things will fade
out, the grooming tugs
and snorts, the winter curl,
and heat stretch, how
she leans her face against
my face and relaxes it there,

like my human things will—
the hair tucking, cake icing,
the pen-to-paper,
and neither of us will mean,
though she means
and means to me now,
and I make her content,
and she me.

Dana Ellyn, *Kitty*

The Other Half of the Simile

They beat him like a dog
They packed them in like cattle
They caged them like animals

And why do we chafe not at the beating,
but which being
is beaten?

Not the cage, but who is caged?

Why should any being be
packed?

They were animals
He was a beast to her

Who are the beasts?

A Garden

The Buddha is crowing
in his beads, which makes
me want to lay my cheek
on his stone middle, but
the poppies won't let me.
They are a salmon
I've never seen in salmon,
and under their wrinkles
purple velour stripes each heart
to make the flies ache,
and the pistil fringes
like a mob of townsfolk
have laid me fetal.
What can I do?

And the poppies and mulch
and Buddha in his beads sigh,
Oh Gretchen, how badly you want
to matter.

CHAIN

You are owned, and you are chained.
The chain stretches from a spike in the
yard to your neck. The yard stretches from
a bare spot behind the house to a barren spot
behind the house. The chain wraps itself
around a paw, deft around an ear, a tail.
Two toes, a leg. The chain spins your body
into a cocoon that spins into a ball, monstrous
metal yarn long enough to knit the earth
a cold straitjacket. In the heart of the ball is you.

Jane O'Hara, *Who Me?*

Thanksgiving

But gentleness is active . . .
will not be driven off . . .
keeps bearing witness calmly.
    —Adrienne Rich

If she tips her face into rain,
she pulls it back down
and tucks toward shelter.

If she's earned her place, her seeds,
the tough bird will take them,
snap for them.

Her body is not dry or stuffed;
not carved, not leftover. It courses
with systems—one that circulates,
sending blood with its sugar and air;

one that reproduces,
composing shell cell
by cool cell, pushing out a life
to wrap in a wing in weather;

one that shoots current
nerve to nerve, shivers
of pleasure in seeds
and heat and children,
alarm when an arm reaches
for her body
to make her body something
carved, something left
over.

POEM BEGINNING WITH A LINE FROM CAM AWKWARD-RICH

I wake up & it breaks my heart.
Two rods of light by the blinds to trap
in my fists & keen for.
All these horses & fish & goats trap my broken
heart. Like you, I was born. Like horses & others I keen
for. Not the soul, which never was.
All these songs wind my heart like a cat's
cradle. Each one mourns & howls
for every animal alive & hardly so.
Each one holds someone born for love
or commerce.

I wake up & find the light, the keening mares & lambs
& notes pinched along these hurt strings.
Like you, I tell everyone with a heart,
I was born.
Like you, the bloodless say,
I kill anyway.
I wake up, see, & it breaks my heart.

MOTHER II

Only humans mother. Only we
care for our babies. Everything
else spits out young. Thank god
you're here, they say, please
rid me of my children. Sell them.
Cage them, kill them. Take
my useless milk. My pups.
Take my eggs. Crack them,
fry them up. Only you mother;
I just lay. Squeeze out. I'm a vessel,
a factory, a vending machine.
Take my young. Profit from them.

FAWN

In the trail lies a body, white spots
big as nickels, hooves small
as dimes. He's so newly dead
the scavengers have just begun
their work: only his muzzle is eaten.

Nature is not kind
or cruel. All beings destroy
to live: camels do, and fawns,
orange newts and their snails.
My dog hovers and sniffs, and I know
what she wants, her tail taut
then trembling, and she knows
what I want, pausing
under *No.*

But I am only a guardian
and take in impure dogs
full of Dog. So I keep on
without her, and when I loop
will see what I see.

Don't Let Him Be Lonely

Beware, even in thought, of assuming the sterile attitude of the spectator, for . . .
a man who wails is not a dancing bear. . . .
—Aimé Césaire

1
Beware of assuming the sterile
attitude of the spectator,
for a dancing bear is not a tool.

2
He does not want to,
not in his body,
his mind, not in any
way, and to watch
is violent, the skirt
is violence,
and the hat, and the bear is a being
who waits for what he knows
he wants, he knows
how to bond and move
and feed and knows none
of these needs is open to him:
he has been made into
spectacle, which is violence.
Beware.

3
The bear may as well be dancing
on hot coals.
The skirt is a skirt of fire,
the jaunty hat lined with thorns.
The chain is linked anvils,
and off stage, the cell is bricked
with ice, floored in burning sand.
A bear.

To Whom I Ate

I'm sorry, steer, for each velvet stack
of pastrami, every burger, the chipped
beef that lay its creamed shoulder on toast.

Birds, I'm sorry for every nugget of you
I bit, every chunk in its crisp salt coat
I dipped in sauce, for dividing
your bodies into "light" and "dark."

I relished you on my tongue, in my
teeth, pushing down my throat and then
churning warm, year after meal

after year. I loved you about to be
served, about to become me, rich
hell, and I'm sorry. You melted
your plush juice into my mouth

and that was my jaw working on
your body, working you into mine.

HALL FARM

You're blackberries—turn black
already. The thorns are in place,
your skin is pebbled, the flowers
you used to be declared you loud
enough to startle toads.

Wind skims the skin from the pond.
Spiders move their kite strings overhead
and the frogs are waving bullhorns.

Orange robin, tangled in the berries,
you're jumping the gun. They aren't
ready yet, though every cell around
tells them different. Jerky little miss,
my stomach is a hot shoe of pollen
and honey. Tell us something from
your jagged beak.

Factory Farms II

We herd lambs into the chute
like Jews herded into
gas like cattle herded
into processing like Angolans
herded onto ships like pigs herded
into factories like soldiers
herded into marches
like calves herded into marches
like Armenians herded into
marches like pigs herded
like Cherokee herded
like cattle herded like Jews

Taste It

I'm a weirdo, eating soup in the rain.
Belching spinach under
an umbrella. *Freak!* say half
the wildflowers. *We'd clamp shut
if we could!* The other half
are mum, clamped shut. How
quickly they widen and pinch,
forming and performing, seeding
and reeling with seeds. *Everyone
I love is dying; when will be
my turn?*
One by one we turn ages. I want to
taste everything once: rain, tiger
lilies, dying tiger lilies, dying.

EGG

Embryo, protein, box, circle, symbol. It came first,
came after, round riddle; proto, almost, plasm.

A hen with wire under her feet, wire at her beak, beak
sliced, wire just above and behind feathers fallen like hair

fallen in bundles, thickets, clumps. Packed in like us packed
in an elevator that will never move again. It smells like that.

It feels like that. Blister it on the gas. Feed on it.
It makes us who we are.

Dana Ellyn, *Kitten Nuggets*

Purple Milkweed II

My work here is done, say
the milkweed cones, drying
and turning dark.
They are too weary to keep
up appearances. They have
fattened the bees, hosted
coupled Monarchs, pushed
out shoots and pulled in
juice: a good life's work. Now
their stems thin and weaken.
Don't be sorry.

UNRAVELING

The times are nightfall, look, their light grows less;
The times are winter, watch, a world undone . . .
—Gerard Manley Hopkins

Summer is late, my heart,
and we are late to its kindnesses.

I want this to become something else,
somewhere kind.

This world is tired.
We sap her juice,

coarsen her skin to cancer.
We heave her children into chutes.

I don't want this to be the night it unravels:
The turtle holding us up

could corrode in poisons:
Turf mows, chemical fires, feedlots—

Summer is late
but may it come, my heart.

Restriction

So this is restriction, this pack of tastes,
the crisp and the dissolving,
the bowl of comfort and bowl of brace,
mashed and crunched, split and whole.
Zippers of wheat, bursting mango,
the tiny skin peeling from a bean,
a hundred plump grains and a hundred plump
nuts, the seeds, the geneses
of tall green stretches and fat green leaves.
That is what becomes my mouth
and body and my heart, and it is
my joy, and plenty.

Jane O'Hara, *Forget Me Not*

NOTES

The epigraphs that begin the book are from Lucille Clifton's *Mercy*, Boa Editions, 2004.

The epigraph of "Coxcomb" is from Greg Kuzma's book *Of China and of Greece*, Sun, 1984.

The first line of "Covid I" is the first line of Lisel Mueller's poem "Magnolia," *Alive Together*, Louisiana State University Press, 1996. (RIP, Lisel Mueller: 1924–2020.)

The epigraph of "Love This" is from Stanley Kunitz's poem "Around Pastor Bonhoeffer," *The Testing Tree*, Little, Brown, 1971.

The epigraph of "God's Glory" is from Edna St. Vincent Millay's play *Conversation at Midnight*, Harper and Brothers, 1937.

The epigraph of "Mercy" is from Walt Whitman's *Democratic Vistas*, Fredonia Books, 2002.

The epigraph of "Factory Farms I" is from Stephen Dunn's poem "At the Restaurant," *Different Hours*, Norton, 2000.

The epigraph of "Heron" is from Gerald Stern's poem "Blacker than Ever," *Odd Mercy*, Norton, 1995.

The epigraph of "Mother I" is from Ben Sollee's album *Dear Companion*, Sub Pop Records, 2010.

The first epigraph of "Big Pig" is from Pablo Neruda's poem "The People," *Plenos Poderes,* New Directions, 1995. The second is from his poem "Bestiary," *Selected Poems,* Houghton Mifflin, 1990.

The title of "When I Got There the Dead Opossum Looked Like" is the first line of Gerald Stern's poem "Behaving Like a Jew," *This Time,* Norton, 1998.

The title of "Apes, May I Speak to You a Moment?" is the first line of Carl Sandburg's poem "Is Wisdom a Lot of Language," *Honey and Salt,* Harcourt, Brace & World, 1963.

The epigraph of "Thanksgiving" is from Adrienne Rich's poem "Natural Resources," *Dream of a Common Language,* Norton, 1993.

The first line of "Poem Beginning with a Line from Cam Awkward-Rich" is the first line of Cameron Awkward-Rich's poem "Meditations in an Emergency," *Dispatch,* Persea Books, 2019.

The title of "Don't Let Him Be Lonely" is taken from Claudia Rankine's *Don't Let Me Be Lonely: An American Lyric* (Norton, 2004), in which she uses Aimé Césaire's quote as an epigraph for one of the poems. I've reused the epigraph here in a pared-down version. Césaire's words come in both cases from *Notebook of a Return to the Native Land,* Wesleyan, 2001.

The epigraph of "Unraveling" is from Gerard Manley Hopkins' poem "The times are nightfall, look, their light grows less," *Poems of Gerard Manley Hopkins,* Humphrey Milford, 1918.

The first line of "Unraveling" is the first line of Kunitz's poem "Touch Me," *Passing Through,* Norton, 1995.

Index of Artwork

ABOUT THE AUTHOR

GRETCHEN PRIMACK is the author of two other collections, *Visiting Days* (Willow Books Editors Select Series 2019), set in a maximum-security men's prison, and *Doris' Red Spaces* (Mayapple Press 2014), as well as an earlier version of *Kind* (Post Traumatic Press 2012). She also co-wrote, with Jenny Brown, *The Lucky Ones: My Passionate Fight for Farm Animals* (Penguin Avery 2013). Her poems have appeared in *The Paris Review, Prairie Schooner, FIELD, Ploughshares, Poet Lore, The Massachusetts Review, The Antioch Review,* and other journals and anthologies. Primack has administrated and taught with college programs and poetry workshops in prison for many years, and she moonlights at an indie bookstore in Woodstock, NY. Reach out to her at www.gretchenprimack.com.

ABOUT THE ARTISTS

DANA ELLYN is a Washington, DC resident and full-time painter who lives and paints in her downtown studio. She has exhibited around the globe with significant museum showings in St. Petersburg, Russia and Baltimore, MD. View and purchase Dana Ellyn's art from her website at www.danaellyn.com.

GUS MUELLER lives in the Hudson Valley and tinkers with bluestone, hollow logs, high-density polyethylene, ghost peppers, snake skins, and microcontrollers. He's been painting since the early 1990s.

JANE O'HARA has participated in solo and group exhibitions with her paintings examining our complex relationship with animals. As both curator of the *Beasts of Burden* exhibition and as an artist, Jane is a Courage of Conscience Award honoree from the Peace Abbey for social justice activism. Her paintings and work with O'Hara Projects can be viewed at www.janeohara.com.

About the Publisher

LANTERN PUBLISHING & MEDIA was founded in 2020 to follow and expand on the legacy of Lantern Books—a publishing company started in 1999 on the principles of living with a greater depth and commitment to the preservation of the natural world. Like its predecessor, Lantern Publishing & Media produces books on animal advocacy, veganism, religion, social justice, and psychology and family therapy. Lantern is dedicated to printing in the United States on recycled paper and saving resources in our day-to-day operations. Our titles are also available as ebooks and audiobooks.

To catch up on Lantern's publishing program, visit us at www.lanternpm.org.

facebook.com/lanternpm
instagram.com/lanternpm
twitter.com/lanternpm